MOLLY'S DELICIOUS

A Play in Two Acts
by
CRAIG WRIGHT

Dramatic Publishing
Woodstock, Illinois • London, England • Melbourne, Australia

*** NOTICE ***

The amateur and stock acting rights to this work are controlled exclusively by THE DRAMATIC PUBLISHING COMPANY without whose permission in writing no performance of it may be given. Royalty fees are given in our current catalog and are subject to change without notice. Royalty must be paid every time a play is performed whether or not it is presented for profit and whether or not admission is charged. A play is performed any time it is acted before an audience. All inquiries concerning amateur and stock rights should be addressed to:

DRAMATIC PUBLISHING
P. O. Box 129, Woodstock, Illinois 60098

COPYRIGHT LAW GIVES THE AUTHOR OR THE AUTHOR'S AGENT *THE EXCLUSIVE RIGHT TO MAKE COPIES.* This law provides authors with a fair return for their creative efforts. Authors earn their living from the royalties they receive from book sales and from the performance of their work. Conscientious observance of copyright law is not only ethical, it encourages authors to continue their creative work. This work is fully protected by copyright. No alterations, deletions or substitutions may be made in the work without the prior written consent of the publisher. No part of this work may be reproduced or transmitted in any form or by any means, electronic or mechanical, including photocopy, recording, videotape, film, or any information storage and retrieval system, without permission in writing from the publisher. It may not be performed either by professionals or amateurs without payment of royalty. All rights, including but not limited to the professional, motion picture, radio, television, videotape, foreign language, tabloid, recitation, lecturing, publication, and reading are reserved.

For performance of any songs and recordings mentioned in this play which are in copyright, the permission of the copyright owners must be obtained or other songs and recordings in the public domain substituted.

©MCMXCVIII by
CRAIG WRIGHT

Printed in the United States of America
All Rights Reserved
(MOLLY'S DELICIOUS)

ISBN 0-87129-884-8

IMPORTANT BILLING AND CREDIT REQUIREMENTS

All producers of the Play *must* give credit to the Author(s) of the Play in all programs distributed in connection with performances of the Play and in all instances in which the title of the Play appears for purposes of advertising, publicizing or otherwise exploiting the Play and/or a production. The name of the Author(s) *must* also appear on a separate line, on which no other name appears, immediately following the title, and *must* appear in size of type not less than fifty percent the size of the title type. Biographical information on the author(s), if included in this book, may be used on all programs. *On all programs this notice must appear:*

"Produced by special arrangement with
THE DRAMATIC PUBLISHING COMPANY of Woodstock, Illinois"

MOLLY'S DELICIOUS

A Play in Two Acts
For 4 Men and 2 Women

CHARACTERS

ALAN (Lindy) LINDA	50s
CINDY LINDA	50s, Lindy's wife
ALISON	18, Cindy's niece
ALEC WILLOUGHBY	18, a mortician's son
JERRY FOUNTAIN	18, in love with Alison
ROSS WILLOUGHBY	50s, Alec's father

TIME: Autumn, 1965.

PLACE: Cindy and Lindy's home
and apple orchard in Pine City, Minn.

Running time: 2 hours and 5 minutes.

MOLLY'S DELICIOUS was premiered by the Arden Theater Company in Philadelphia, September 30, 1997. The production was directed by Aaron Posner, with sets by Chris Pickert; costumes by Bonnie Doyle; lighting by Andrew Billiau; and sound by James Murphy. The cast was as follows:

Alan (Lindy) Linda	TOM TETI
Cindy	MARCIA SAUNDERS
Alison	MAGGIE SIFF
Alec	DAVID BARDEEN
Jerry	IAN MERRILL PEAKES
Ross	HARRY BERGMAN

For Louis and Lorraine

ACT ONE

AT RISE: *It's late on a Sunday morning. LINDY picks apples, dropping them into a shoulder bag, and ROSS and LINDY talk while CINDY sets up an easel.*

ROSS. Lindy, what in heaven's name are you gonna do with all these apples?
LINDY. Ross, I got no god-blessed idea. And now the weatherman says the frost is on the way?
ROSS. By the end of the week, he said.
LINDY. I suppose down at the funeral home you're getting as many bodies as you can into the ground before the big freeze-up, right?
ROSS *(confused).* No...
CINDY. You have to forgive him, Ross, he thinks he's funny but he's not.
ROSS. His column in the paper's always good for a hoot.
CINDY. Don't encourage him. *(CINDY takes ROSS aside and sets him on a bench and starts posing him this way and that, stepping back, eyeing the picture, trying again.)*
ROSS. Lindy, your column's the only reason I get that stupid paper anymore. Mike Nelson should just face it, there's no news in Pine City, he oughta get back to printing phone books, that operation in Wadena—did you hear, every other page of the Fergus Falls phone

book's upside down? And, meanwhile, Vonda Porkonnen's hot-dish recipe is front-page news! There's nothing happening here, people should just shut up! So, Cindy, everyone down to Sundberg's been asking, what are you gonna do with all these apples?

CINDY. We're eating as many as we can. I've sent Heather and Susan each a box for their families, and Kjersten one up to college. I've put up a whole pantry full of applesauce. The root cellar's stuffed, and it's only a drop in the bucket, the trees are still full of apples.

ROSS *(to LINDY).* Why in heaven's name did you plant so many trees?

LINDY. I didn't expect every damn tree to survive.

ROSS. What happens if you just let them fall to the ground?

LINDY. Oh, it's a god-awful mess, you slip and fall on your ass every five steps you take. *(Setting a bushel in front of ROSS.)* Happy Rosh Hashanah.

ROSS. But I'm not—

LINDY. Nobody ever said you were, Ross, that's just what it is.

(LINDY pours his shoulder bag of apples into a basket near ROSS. CINDY, meanwhile, has established ROSS in a "dignified" pose. She steps back, eyes the picture. LINDY just stands there. CINDY begins drawing ROSS with pastels.)

CINDY *(to ROSS).* You didn't happen to see the northern lights last night, did you?

ROSS. No.

CINDY. Oh they were just gorgeous.

ROSS. I heard that from Clem Vogt, he saw 'em out at his place.

CINDY. They were, they were absolutely gorgeous. Angel wings and forms stretched out, Ross, it was—oh my—it was like watching a symphony orchestra in the sky!

ROSS. Thanks to Mayor Ed's fancy new streetlights, we can't even see the stars in town anymore.

CINDY. Then I tell you what, we'll have you out soon. Lindy?

LINDY *(nodding)*. Yep.

CINDY. We'll have you out for some dinner and natural darkness, Ross, how about that?

ROSS. I'd like that very much.

CINDY. And tell you what, you could bring your boy, Alec—that'd be nice, maybe? A little change of pace for you two bachelors? *(Silence. LINDY is standing there, chomping loudly on an apple.)* Was there something more you had to say or can you go now?

LINDY. Listen, Ross, if you've got the entrepreneurial bug and you want to give away a bushel with every burial as a sort of promotion incentive, I'd be happy to drop my price.

ROSS *(to CINDY)*. He's charging me for these?

CINDY *(eternally unamused)*. No.

LINDY. I just don't like to see anything go to waste, Ross, so, absolutely free, as much as you want.

ROSS. I'll keep that in mind. *(LINDY lingers.)*

CINDY. Don't you have to talk to a man about a horse or something?

LINDY. No, do you? *(To ROSS.)* See, my theory is she wants me to leave because she's planning on killing me and she wants you to do the arrangements, because after all that poison, a natural look is gonna be so important.

CINDY. Just go away!

LINDY. I'm going. *(To ROSS.)* You be careful. *(LINDY exits into the orchard. CINDY immediately puts down her pastels and joins ROSS on the bench.)*

CINDY. Listen. I didn't ask you out here to talk about apples, Ross. Or about killing my husband, although it's not such a bad idea. But first, can you promise not to tell Lindy we talked?

ROSS *(taking her hand empathetically)*. I understand.

CINDY. No, no, Ross, it's nothing like that—no funerals! It's about Alison.

ROSS. Your niece.

CINDY. She's pregnant.

ROSS *(lying)*. Really? I hadn't heard.

CINDY. What a gentleman.

ROSS. So her young officer hasn't come calling yet?

CINDY. No. And between you and me, he's not going to, either.

ROSS. You don't think so?

CINDY. No. He's been shipped out to Vietnam, and from the little Alison's told me about him, I don't see much cause for hope.

ROSS. What has she said?

CINDY. Oh, just what you'd expect: he's very handsome and charming and he has lots of prospects.

ROSS. That doesn't sound so bad.

CINDY. Then where the heck is he? She's been writing him once a week at his APO, and the boy hasn't written back, not ONCE! And every day she's down there at that mailbox, WAITING...

Act I   MOLLY'S DELICIOUS   11

ROSS. I see your point.
CINDY. But, I've heard from a pretty reliable source that somebody we know might actually have some feelings towards her.
ROSS. Who?
CINDY. Alec.
ROSS. MY Alec?
CINDY. Mmhmm. *(Brief pause.)*
ROSS. Feelings?
CINDY. Mmhmm.
ROSS. Towards Alison?
CINDY. That's what I heard.
ROSS. From who?
CINDY. So you don't think it's true?
ROSS. Who'd you hear that from?
CINDY *(after a pregnant pause)*. May Whipstadt.
ROSS. Jiminy Christmas, that woman is a talker! Do you know that if she has her way, Dwayne Lund is going to get arrested for having Mafia connections!
CINDY. Little Dwayne Lund at the Sandwich Hut?
ROSS. Yes! The sheriff doesn't want to take him in, but May's got everybody so stirred up now, he's gonna have to!
CINDY. Dwayne Lund and the Mafia? But that's absolutely absurd!
ROSS. Tell May Whipstadt! She sits at that piano during Rotary lunch and holds court on everything that isn't any of her business!
CINDY. So you think she's wrong about Alec?
ROSS. How should I know? That boy doesn't talk to me. And did you hear Tom Pedersen's selling his house and

moving to Norway just to get away from Mavis Luneburg!

CINDY. No!

ROSS. Yes! Word is Tom's, *(Shaking his hand in the air.)* you know, so. And since Larry's gone, Mavis has lost all the sense she ever had which isn't much, and Don Hummel says he's actually seen Mavis banging on Tom's windows at night, and sneaking around! It's an out and out obsession! And in the middle of Jackie David's piano lesson Friday last, Mavis burst into tears in the middle of "Für Elise" and scared the poor girl out of her wits, that's what I heard.

CINDY. From who?

ROSS *(after a beat)*. May Whipstadt. But THAT story at least has a ring of truth to it—everyone knows about Tom, you know, so, and Mavis! But Dwayne Lund and the Mafia!? You can't even get Italian food in this town, let alone connections!

CINDY. Well, May told me Ardy Hanson said Alec's had his eye on Alison.

ROSS. I can't imagine that being true, Cindy, the boy doesn't think about anything but work.

CINDY. Even so, would you have a word with him?

ROSS. She's a nice girl?

CINDY. Oh sure, she just made a little mistake, Ross, that's all. She deserves a second chance.

ROSS. She wouldn't want to take him back East with her, would she? Because I couldn't let that happen. I'd be up Sugar Creek without a paddle if I didn't have Alec. The Willoughbys have been burying Pine City for sixty-seven years—

CINDY. Why don't we just cross that bridge when we come to it, Ross? We don't even KNOW yet if the boy's in love with her.

ROSS. "In love with her"!?

CINDY. That's what I heard.

ROSS. Jiminy Christmas! "Feelings"! I wish his mother were still alive to screw up this sort of thing. *(In the distance, we can hear the low rumble and whistle of the train going through town. CINDY gets up and finishes drawing ROSS.)*

CINDY. I'm sure you'll do just fine. I have to go get the—psst—for the picture—listen, if you talk to Alec and everything works out, have him come out for some pie.

ROSS. Well, maybe next week I'll do that.

CINDY. Actually, about an hour from now would be best; and listen, Ross, this is between you and me.

ROSS. Of course!

CINDY. I mean it!

ROSS. I mean it too!

CINDY. Good.

ROSS. You and Lindy really should consider making some funeral arrangements, you know.

CINDY. I know we should, Ross—

ROSS. Nobody lives forever—

CINDY. Nobody does, I know—

ROSS. You could be dead this time tomorrow—

CINDY. Thank you, I'll keep that in mind when I'm grocery shopping. Listen! Whatever you do, you CAN'T tell Lindy we talked.

ROSS. Why not?

CINDY. Because if you do, I'll burn your house down!

(CINDY exits into the house. ROSS admires his portrait a moment, and then LINDY enters, with an apron full of apples.)

LINDY. You and Cindy have a nice talk, Ross?

ROSS. No!

LINDY. No?

ROSS. No, I mean, yes, but about anything, no, nothing, nice, no.

LINDY. Ross, you know that Billy kid at Lindberg's garage?

ROSS. Yeah?

LINDY. I heard Kathy Larsen has him spending the night whenever Eric's out to Watertown on oil business.

ROSS. No!

LINDY. I know it!

ROSS. He worked on my car!

LINDY. Mine too! And he did a fine job! I guess now we know where he's getting his chops. And if Eric didn't have that little piece of business in Watertown keeping him warm at night, I'd be tempted to tell him, too!

ROSS. No!

LINDY. Yes!

ROSS. Where did you hear THAT?

LINDY. May Whipstadt.

ROSS. OH, that woman is a talker!

LINDY. Yep.

ROSS. It's a wonder anybody gets away with anything in this town when that woman's mouth can't hold a word in it for more than ten seconds before she's spitting it out again! Speaking of which, Lindy, do you think

Dwayne Lund could in any way, shape, or form have Mafia connections?

LINDY. Little Dwayne Lund down at the Sandwich Hut?

ROSS. That's what May's been telling everybody.

LINDY. That boy's hardly got nerve endings, Ross, how could he have Mafia connections?

ROSS. See, that's what I think too, but Walt says he's gonna have to bring him in just to stop a panic.

LINDY. No.

ROSS. Yes! She's whipping everybody up! And you know what else I heard, and this hits pretty close to home, turns out my own boy, Alec's, got a thing for your little niece, Alison! *(Brief pause. ROSS catches himself.)* OH CRIPES! I gotta go.

LINDY. Keep it on the straight and narrow, Ross.

ROSS. You too, Lindy, and listen, you and Cindy should really think about making some arrangements—

LINDY. I won't tell Cindy you told me.

ROSS. Thank you!

(ROSS exits. CINDY enters from the house and with an aerosol can.)

CINDY. Where'd Ross get to?

LINDY. He, uh...had to run.

CINDY. Really?

LINDY. Yep. Something...came up. In conversation.

CINDY *(playing it cool)*. That silly goose. If he'd just waited a second, he could have taken his picture with. *(CINDY sprays the picture with fixative and then begins putting away her art supplies.)*

LINDY. Cindy.

CINDY. What?

LINDY. If you honestly think—

CINDY *(overlapping)*. Oh, stop it—

LINDY *(continuing)*. —for one minute I don't know what you're doing, having Ross and Alec out for dinner, then living with me all these years has driven you even crazier than I thought. You don't have any damn right meddling in that girl's affairs!

CINDY. Lindy, that girl's affairs need meddling like a cake needs eggs! She is throwing her life down the toilet waiting for that boy! He's not coming and that's all there is to it!

LINDY. You know he's not coming...?

CINDY *(looking off towards where ROSS exited)*. Did Ross tell you we talked?

LINDY. You don't KNOW he's not coming!

CINDY. Did Ross tell you we talked?

LINDY. NO!

CINDY. Oh, the mouth on that man!

LINDY *(referring to ALEC)*. So, see, maybe he is!

CINDY. He's as bad as May!

LINDY. Cindy, just imagine for a second, what toilet your life would have been thrown down, OK, if your mom had gotten it into her head while I was overseas to make you marry Rusty Carnook!

CINDY *(vaguely remembering)*. The Fish Boy?

LINDY. With the boogers, yeah, Rusty Carnook. Remember him? Sitting there on that stool in his driveway every summer, working on that snowmobile—picking his nose?

CINDY. Lindy, Alec Willoughby is no Rusty Carnook.

LINDY. Just imagine it, though. Imagine yourself with HIM. Feeding his mean little rabbit. Bringing him that stinky apple cider vinegar he always used to drink. Imagine life without me.

CINDY. You don't know what kind of danger you're putting yourself in, mister.

LINDY. JUST with Rusty Carnook!

CINDY. Ok, I'm imagining it.

LINDY *(making a "boogery" face)*. You, Rusty Carnook, and all those fat green boogers.

CINDY. Lindy, do you honestly think you're Albert Einstein?

LINDY. I'm just making a point.

CINDY. I know, but you should see the look on your face.

LINDY. My point is, if the girl's in love—

CINDY. And while she's in love, who'll raise that baby? Her? You? Because it isn't going to be me, Lindy, I'm done raising children.

LINDY. But maybe this what's his name'll show up!

CINDY. Oh right, a man shows up! Give me a break!

LINDY. It'd be your niece.

CINDY. GREAT-niece, you idiot, and I don't care! My life is finally my own for the first time in twenty-six years. Twenty-six years of nothing but—

LINDY. Wonderful times.

CINDY. Yes, but thank God they're finally over!

LINDY. If the girls could hear you talk this way—

CINDY. There'd be a problem, you're right, because they'd still be living at home! Lindy, I can finally see the light at the end of our long tunnel of daughters. Heather and Susan are married. Kjersty's safe at college. This autumn, Lindy—this one right here—was supposed to be mine! Just mine! Now, you changed your life, you sold your hardware store, planted your apple trees! Well, the girls are all grown up now and there're things I want to do, OK? Me! Just me!

LINDY. Like what?

CINDY. Oh, don't you dare say it that way!

LINDY. Like how?

CINDY. Like you just did, "like what"! Like it would be such a miracle if I got an idea!

LINDY. Sorry. "Like what"?

CINDY. I don't know. Learn Italian maybe.

LINDY. Italian? What do you need to know Italian for?

CINDY. Or open a little shop in town to sell my pictures, would that be so strange? Pam Schmit and I have been talking about maybe opening somewhere in town, a place where we could sell all the things local people make, and maybe have a little art gallery.

LINDY *(incredulous)*. In Pine City, Minnesota?

CINDY. Don't look at me that way, Lindy, it's a *good* idea.

LINDY. I'm sure it is, but if it came to marrying Alison off to some stinky little mortician or raising that baby—

CINDY. Lindy, my stupid sister, Miss High and Mighty, won't take her back without a husband! Now if you want to change the diapers for two years and pay for another education, then you do it, but I am done raising children.

LINDY. All right, I'll make it simple for you. If you set that lively young girl up with that stinky little mortician, I swear, Cindy, I am never gonna say another damn word to you ever again.

CINDY. Lucky, lucky me.

LINDY. I mean it! That girl's life is NOT some dusty corner that needs a little straightening up, it's a LIFE. And it's HERS. And whether she's wrong to wait for this what's his name or not, she certainly deserves better than that little mortician, and you know it!

CINDY. Lindy, you're wrong about Alec.

LINDY. You think he's as good as she deserves?

CINDY. I don't know who deserves what in this world and neither do you. *(Brief pause.)*

LINDY. So that's it?

CINDY. Yes, that's it!

LINDY. You're just gonna set her up with that stinky little embalmer.

CINDY. No one's setting anyone up, Lindy, we're having him over for PIE!

LINDY. Oh, you make it sound so innocent.

CINDY. If it sounds so innocent, maybe it is! Did you ever think about that?

LINDY. All right. I've said what's true and you're not interested. Alison's in love with this what's his name and the chips oughta be free to fall where they may, because that's what life is for. But you want it this way, so this is how you'll get it, Cindy, draw your pretty little picture and I'll just watch it blow away!

CINDY *(overlapping).* Lindy, I don't want anything any way—

LINDY. You just better remember this moment, because THIS is the last word you're ever gonna hear out of my mouth. *(Brief pause.)*

CINDY. "This" or "mouth"?

LINDY. Neither! "You don't mess with true love."

CINDY. You know that's six words, you're aware of that, right?

LINDY *(as he goes)*. Yes! *(LINDY exits into orchard.)*

CINDY *(screaming)*. There, that's better! "True love," no, but "Yes"—that's a silence I can live with!

(CINDY exits, with easel and supplies, into the house. Time passes. ALISON enters, finds a seat on the front porch and reads a letter out loud to herself.)

ALISON. Dear Jerry. Hi. It's me. Alison. Again. Wondering how you're doing. Are you OK? It's autumn here in Minnesota, and it's already started to get cold at night— the sky has that clear black look to it, like it goes on forever. And the leaves on the maple trees, they're as red as the apples on the apple trees. But the leaves on the apple trees, they stay green all year. Did you know that? My Uncle Lindy is going absolutely crazy trying to figure out what he's going to do with all his apples—he thinks he'll have more than ten thousand before the snow falls! Wouldn't that be a pie? I wear your sweatshirt all the time. Aunt Cindy's made me wash it once or twice but it still smells a little like you. And when I wear it, if I shut my eyes and wrap my arms around myself really tight, it's almost like I'm in your arms again. Almost. I know it must be hard for you, too, to be away for so long—not just from me, but from everyone you love. So when are you coming home? And do they play "the Beatles" on Armed Forces Radio? Every time I hear "P.S. I Love You," I want to sit down and write you a letter. Or get one? Oh, Jerry, I want to hear you sing to me again and hold your hand and be your little firecracker, so please hurry back when you can. Sincerely, Alison. P.S. I love you. Ha ha.

(She folds the letter, kisses it, slips it into an envelope. CINDY enters from the house, having seen ALISON through the window.)

CINDY. Baby, what on earth are you doing out here?

ALISON. Nothing.

CINDY. I've been looking all over the house for you. Come here.

ALISON. What is it?

CINDY. I want to brush your hair, you look like some sort of wild animal.

ALISON. I am a wild animal. *(CINDY sits beside ALISON and begins brushing ALISON's hair.)*

CINDY. Was that a letter to Jerry?

ALISON. Yes.

CINDY. Baby, why on earth do you want to break your heart hoping for this boy to show up, when it looks so awfully unlikely that he will?

ALISON. I must not think it's so "awfully unlikely."

CINDY. You really don't?

ALISON. Aunt Cindy, the bond between me and Jerry maybe runs a little bit deeper than you're used to, OK?

CINDY. But you write the boy letters, Ali, and he never writes back!

ALISON. I don't need "a letter" to know he loves me!

CINDY. But you've told him you're pregnant and he hasn't even—

ALISON. No I haven't! *(Brief pause. ALISON's hair is now up in a bun. CINDY takes out some blush and eyeliner and begins making up ALISON's face.)*

CINDY. Excuse me?

ALISON. I haven't told him.

CINDY. You haven't told him you're pregnant?

ALISON. No!

CINDY. And WHY NOT?

ALISON. Because he doesn't have to marry me just for the baby!

CINDY. Yes he DOES!

ALISON. No, he doesn't, would you stop being so old-fashioned!

CINDY. But Alison, that baby is your only hope of him ever coming back, don't you see that?

ALISON. No! If Jerry comes back, he'll come back for ME.

CINDY. Well, I'm really sorry to tell you this, baby, and it's got nothing to do with you, but he won't.

ALISON *(bravado)*. All right then, he won't! *(Brief pause.)* He promised he would!

CINDY. A man's promise and five cents will get you a cup of coffee.

ALISON. But you don't know, Aunt Cindy, Jerry's different.

CINDY. They're *all* different, baby, and they're *all* the same. Does your mother know you haven't told him about this?

ALISON. Don't you call her!

CINDY. Don't YOU use that tone with ME, little lady!

ALISON. I mean it, don't call her. Please?

CINDY. I don't believe you! You've got everyone so worried about this and you haven't even told the boy you're pregnant, Lord above! You get in the house right now and make the call!

ALISON. No!

CINDY. Yes, you GET! Now!

ALISON. NO!

CINDY. Baby, someone's got to tell this boy what he's done to you!

ALISON. No one has DONE anything to me, Aunt Cindy, I'm just pregnant! *(Brief pause.)*

CINDY. Well that settles it right there, you have obviously lost all your little marbles.

ALISON. Listen to me. If you, or my mother, or anybody calls up Jerry and tells him I'm pregnant and he *has* to marry me, our whole life together will never be anything more than a prison sentence, don't you see that? My whole life'll be wasted, wondering if he ever really loved me or not. Hoping he might learn to. And all the time his bitterness making him uglier and uglier, which would be a real shame, Aunt Cindy, because he is such a beautiful man. But, if he does come back for me like he said he would, then at least I KNOW what I've got. I know I've got someone who thinks I'm special. Someone who can't settle for anyone else but me. Someone whose prayers I and I alone can answer just by being who I am. That's how I want to be loved. *(Brief pause. CINDY strategically decides to capitulate.)*

CINDY. Then I won't call your mother.

ALISON. Thank you.

(They start exiting peacefully together into the house as LINDY brings on a basket of apples.)

CINDY. On one condition. *(They exit. We hear them talking very quietly as they go.)* There's this boy from town I'd like you to meet named Alec Willoughby.
ALISON. Aunt Cindy, don't set me up, please. *(LINDY, meanwhile, whistling to himself, starts filling the apple press with apples.)*
CINDY. I'm not setting you up, would you stop being so suspicious! He's just a very nice young man, about your age, who helps people out with their...funerals and stuff...
ALISON. A mortician?!!
CINDY. No!!

(We hear ALISON scream. She comes running back on through the front door.)

ALISON. Uncle Lindy, help me, please! I don't want to meet a mortician!

(CINDY enters from the house.)

CINDY. Baby, he's not a mortician!
ALISON *(to LINDY)*. Is Alec Willoughby a mortician?
LINDY. Of course he's a mortician, he comes from a long line of morticians.
ALISON *(to CINDY)*. I don't believe you would try to set me up with a mortician, what are you thinking?
CINDY. Baby, he's a very sweet young man.
LINDY *(to ALISON)*. Sweet smelling.
CINDY. I thought you weren't talking to me!
LINDY *(to CINDY)*. I'm not, am I? I'm not! *(To ALISON.)* He smells like one of those frogs from the Mason jar.

CINDY. You think you're funny but—
LINDY. I AM! And YOU are the hole that the humor in this house drains out of!
CINDY. Oh, really? Well, I'm sorry if raising you and your children has taken the wit out of my sails, but that doesn't give you the right to screw up this girl's last chance at a decent life making jokes at that boy's expense! He can't help that he was born in that family, I'm sure he's doing his best. *(To ALISON.)* Don't think of him as a mortician, baby, think of him as a funeral director.
LINDY *(to ALISON)*. There, that makes it all better, doesn't it.
ALISON. Aunt Cindy, if he comes over here, I swear I'll hang myself. *(We hear a car pull up offstage.)*
LINDY. The rope's in the basement.
CINDY. Cheese and rice!
ALISON. Is that him?
CINDY. Please, baby, just give him a chance, he's come all this way—
ALISON. I'm gonna go hang myself.
LINDY. Remember, you're heavier than usual, so think it through. *(ALISON exits into the house, slamming the door behind her.)* This is all so romantic.
CINDY. Lindy, when this is all over, you and I are going to have either a very long talk or a very short gunfight.

(CINDY exits into the house. LINDY fills the apple press with apples as ALEC enters, holding a small bouquet of wildflowers.)

ALEC. Good afternoon, Mr. Linda.

LINDY. Good afternoon, Mr. Willoughby. You can call me "Lindy."

ALEC. Sir, I know this'll seem old-fashioned, but I've never been that comfortable calling my elders by their given names.

LINDY. And I've never been that comfortable with anyone calling me "Mr. Linda." It's an unfortunate Finnish name, Alec. I wear it with shame. There's no point in dwelling on it.

ALEC. If you hate it so much, why don't you change it?

LINDY. For all intents and purposes, Alec, I have. Call me "Lindy."

ALEC. Yes sir.

LINDY. Lindy.

ALEC. Lindy.

LINDY. You want an apple?

ALEC. No, thank you, sir, I just brushed my teeth.

LINDY. Then I'll set you up with a bushel when you go.

ALEC. We've still got a whole bushel at home, sir.

LINDY. What's the matter, you don't like apples?

ALEC. No sir, I like them. I'd take another bushel.

LINDY. Good. *(Brief pause.)* Those wouldn't happen to be funeral flowers, would they?

ALEC. No. That'd be kind of creepy anyway, wouldn't it?

LINDY. That's exactly what I was gonna say. *(Brief pause.)* What did you think of Pastor Ed's sermon this morning?

ALEC. I don't know.

LINDY. He's lobbying pretty hard for that shopping mall, don't you think?

ALEC. I guess so.

LINDY. If I were him, I'd be ashamed, I mean, three Sundays in a row now he's twisted the Gospel into an argument on behalf of that monstrosity.

ALEC. They're saying there'd be a Chinese restaurant.

LINDY. Yeah, well, I don't like Chinese food much, do you?

ALEC. I like it OK.

LINDY. And I suppose you think church is a place for playing politics too?

ALEC. No—

LINDY. And streetlights all over town, that was his idea too, wasn't it? You like the streetlights?

ALEC. No!

LINDY. He shouldn't've brought out that blueprint, Alec! The altar's no place for a blueprint!

ALEC. I—I agree. *(Brief pause.)*

LINDY. You got a draft card?

ALEC. Yes sir.

LINDY. That's good.

ALEC. Is Alison here?

LINDY. Why do you want to know? *(For an instant, we hear CINDY and ALISON yelling at each other in the house.)*

CINDY *(offstage)*. Young lady, you will not wear that Coast Guard sweatshirt!

ALISON *(offstage)*. I'll wear whatever I want, you old weirdo!

CINDY *(offstage)*. You will not, and don't you dare talk to me that way!

ALISON *(offstage)*. I wish I was dead!

CINDY *(offstage)*. I wish you were too, at least then I could get you dressed! *(Sound of breaking glass. LINDY slides the cap on and begins slowly screwing down the press.)*

LINDY. Girl talk. Look, Alec, do you really have any— feelings towards Alison?

ALEC. What do you mean, sir?

LINDY. I mean I assume you've got intentions, coming here, Alec, but do you actually have any feelings for Alison?

ALEC. I don't really know her that well, yet, sir, to say.

LINDY. No, you don't, do you?

ALEC. I do think she's very pretty, though.

LINDY. "Pretty"?

ALEC. Yes sir.

LINDY. "Pretty."

ALEC. I think she's easily the prettiest girl in town.

LINDY. And what about Wanda Jensen? I thought she was the prettiest girl in town.

ALEC. Oh, Wanda's got nothing on Alison.

LINDY. You're putting me on.

ALEC. No sir. Lindy.

LINDY. What's the matter, Wanda's not your type?

ALEC. Wanda would be kind of pretty, I guess, if she got that look off her face. But I think Alison's prettier.

LINDY. That's not really very much to build a relationship on, though, is it?—thinking someone's pretty. Kind of an immature way to get the ball rolling, if you ask me. When I met Cindy, I didn't think she was pretty at all, but I admired, very deeply, her mind.

ALEC. If I could go in, I'd get started at least—

LINDY. No, wait, tell me something else. If you think Alison's so pretty, Alec, why haven't you ever been out here to visit before? She's been here all summer long—

ALEC. I guess I figured she wasn't available.
LINDY. Why?
ALEC. Because of, uh, I don't know—
LINDY. Because of her big tummy?
ALEC. Yes sir.
LINDY. You're not really very committed, are you?
ALEC. Sir—
LINDY. You obviously must not think she's that pretty!
ALEC. Sir, why are you making this so hard for me?
LINDY. I don't know how many dates you've been on, Alec, but when a boy comes calling on a girl, the man of the house gets to do whatever he wants to the boy. That's nature's way. *(We hear the sound of glass breaking and then the sound of CINDY and ALISON fighting fades in from offstage.)*
ALISON *(offstage).* That's what I think of your stupid old poodle skirt, you weirdo!
CINDY *(offstage).* Do you talk to your mother this way?
ALISON *(offstage).* Do you set your daughters up with morticians?
CINDY *(offstage).* Oh, don't try that fancy logic on me, little lady, it won't work! *(Another glass object is heard breaking offstage.)*
LINDY. Do you think there's any chance you'll ever be leaving the funeral business, Alec?
ALEC. No sir.
LINDY. See, now, that's too bad. That's too bad for YOU. Because I'll be honest with you, Alec, Alison is a great girl. She's smart as a whip and she leads with her heart. And you're right, she IS the prettiest girl in this town; Wanda Jensen oughta get that look off her face, you're a very perceptive young man.

ALEC. Thank you.

LINDY. So let me be straight with you again. My wife doesn't have any right getting involved in Alison's affairs. They're nobody's business but hers. And while you do seem like a decent young man, Alec, even if you were Spartacus, I don't think I could ever stand by and let Alison marry into your family, where breakfast, lunch and dinner are always right before a damn funeral!

ALEC. The decision is hers, though, right?

LINDY *(caught off guard)*. "Hers"? What do you mean?

ALEC. Well, like you said, sir, this is an affair of the heart, and it's nobody's business but hers. Like you said. Right?

LINDY. Of course. I mean, you're here, aren't you? I'm not about to throw you out. She is, but I'm not. By the way, did you see *Spartacus*?

ALEC. No sir.

LINDY. It's really a heck of a movie.

(ALISON and CINDY from the house.)

ALISON. Hi.

ALEC. Hello.

ALISON. I'm Alison.

ALEC. I'm Alec.

ALISON. I'm pregnant.

ALEC. These are for you.

ALISON *(takes the flowers)*. Thanks. Listen—I don't know what my Aunt Cindy's told you—but Jerry?—the father of my baby?—he's in the Coast Guard?—in Vietnam?—and he's going to come for me as soon as he gets discharged and then we're going to get married—so I want you to know how much I appreciate this gesture—coming out here?—it's very sweet and old-fashioned of you—but the old days are really gone, aren't they?—they kind of are—and you don't really know me or love me or anything and you wouldn't want some other man's baby anyway, so thanks. Really. Thanks. But no thanks, I guess. You know? No, thanks. But thanks. Goodbye. *(ALISON hands him his flowers and exits into the house. Long silence. Then:)*

CINDY. Alec, I'm sorry I asked you to come today. I guess I'm just a nosey Parker and I should've minded my own business. Alison's set on wasting her life waiting for this Coast Guard boy and nothing any of us sensible people say is going to change her mind. I just want you to know it's got nothing to do with you being a mortician. We all think you're a very brave young man, Alec, to do what you do, and you'll never get anything but respect from us about it. Now I'll feel like a real fool if you don't at least come in and have a piece of pie.

ALEC. No, Mrs. Linda, thank you.

CINDY. Oh, come on, just say yes.

(ALISON enters and goes right to ALEC.)

ALISON. Alec, do you wish these weirdoes would just leave you the hell alone?

ALEC. Yes.

ALISON. Good, because I do too. Goodbye, weirdoes! *Goodbye! (After a pause, CINDY and LINDY start to exit.)*

CINDY *(sotto voce, "I told you so")*. You see that? You see?

LINDY. I'm not talking to you! *(CINDY and LINDY exit. ALISON and ALEC share a few uncomfortable moments. Finally, ALISON breaks the ice by tossing ALEC an apple. A peaceful, amiable silence, the kind only young people are comfortable with, is established before the scene continues.)*

ALISON. These apples are all Molly's Delicious. This apple grower in Wisconsin, way way back before World War I, "developed" it, I guess, as a tribute to Molly, the girl of his dreams. He took a branch from a Red Delicious and grafted it onto a Keepsake, and after two years of trial and error, created this apple with the highest sugar content of any apple ever grown in America. And with a basket of those apples, the first Molly's Delicious picked from the first crop ever, he showed up at her door and proposed. No one believes in love like that anymore, Alec. No one!

ALEC. I do.

ALISON. I do too. But nobody else does, you know? They've all given up and they want us to give up too, because our faith reminds them of their failures, which they want to forget. Isn't that sick? It's so sick. I want you to know I'm not mad at you, Alec, I don't blame *you* for glumping out here and pestering me, I know it wasn't your idea. The way I see it, you're just like me, we're in this together. We're two young people with natural dreams who are about to be fed into a giant crunching gearbox because nobody can stand to have us around if our hearts aren't broken. Do you know what I mean?

ALEC. I do.

ALISON. I know you do, Alec, because you're a good person. That's the only reason I'm out here with you, I could tell right away you were a good person, and I didn't want to let their sick, secret plan rob us of our chance to be friends, you know, because we deserve it. We of all people should get something out of this stupid situation, just to show them, you know? Just to remind them where it's at. Alec, I have more hope and imagination in my little finger than the whole ugly world put together, do you know what that's like?

ALEC. No.

ALISON. It's really lonely.

ALEC. I know what THAT'S like.

ALISON. Great. Then we'll be friends. This is great. Friends?

ALEC. Friends. *(They shake hands.)*

ALISON. So do you have a girlfriend?

ALEC. No. What would I be doing out here if I had a girlfriend?

ALISON. I don't know. Good point. I guess I assumed you were just being noble.

ALEC. No, I'm not noble, I'm lonely, remember? You don't know this, but I saw you at Bess Hummel's wedding.

ALISON. Back when I first got here?

ALEC. Yeah, and I was asking everybody who you were, and what you were doing in town, and they were all saying, "Get out, she's too pretty for you."

ALISON. I'm not too pretty for you.

ALEC. Technically you are, yeah.

ALISON. No!

ALEC. Yeah, technically.

ALISON. You're a handsome guy, Alec. Don't shortchange yourself. This might be an awful thing to say, but when I heard you were a, you know, what you do?—I was expecting Boris Karloff meets Jim Nabors. Or a really pale Bobby Goldsboro. I was really surprised you were so nice-looking.

ALEC. Thanks.

ALISON. I mean it, it was a BIG surprise.

ALEC. Thanks.

ALISON. Could you tell at the wedding I was carrying this little cannonball around?

ALEC. No, you looked beautiful. You look beautiful now, too, I mean... You do. Is that too strange, should I not say that? Are you not supposed to be beautiful when you're pregnant? Is there some...rule...? *(Brief pause.)*

ALISON. You really don't have a girlfriend, Alec?

ALEC. Why?

ALISON. This is amazing to me.

ALEC. Come on.

ALISON. No, it is!

ALEC. Girls don't fall in love with morticians.

ALISON. Oh, that can't be true.

ALEC. It is.

ALISON. But it can't be! There must be morticians with girlfriends. I bet I've seen morticians with girlfriends.

ALEC. When have you even seen a mortician before now?

ALISON. No, I bet I've seen one without knowing it, and when I did, he was with a girl.

ALEC. Well, it wasn't me.

ALISON. So then why do you do it? You're a nice-looking guy, you'd have no trouble getting a girl.

ALEC. I know.

ALISON. Oh, you know?

ALEC. Yes, I know!

ALISON. Oh, he knows! Well well well, he knows!

ALEC. I mean, YOU are technically too pretty for me, but I know that I'm nice-looking enough that if I wasn't a mortician I could at least get somebody!

ALISON. But you don't want just somebody, do you? You want the girl of your dreams!

ALEC. Right!

ALISON. And you're never gonna get her if you're a mortician!

ALEC. Probably not! Right!

ALISON. So why do you do it?

ALEC. I'll tell you. It's really simple. I do it because Pine City is a very small town, there's only one funeral home here, and my father owns it.

ALISON. But then you should quit!

ALEC. Are you crazy?

ALISON. No, this is classic, you're young and you're in love and you want out of the family business! Quit!

ALEC. If I quit, Alison, my father would die.

ALISON. I have some news for you, Chester, he's gonna die either way. Aren't any of your brothers creepy enough to—

ALEC. I don't have any brothers. And my dad wants to retire soon. And no one else in town is about to learn how to deal with a dead body. This is Pine City, Minnesota, Alison, not Connecticut. These people can't pick where to have their arrangements made. There's the Willoughby Funeral Home and that's it.

ALISON. But, Alec, you can't waste your life doing something you don't want to do.

ALEC. Everybody around here does.

ALISON. Yeah, but not everybody does something so *disgusting*.

ALEC. It's not that disgusting.

ALISON. Oh, it must be, come on, dead bodies?!

ALEC. Death is just part of life.

ALISON. Oh, you don't really believe that, do you?

ALEC. I think I do...

ALISON. Death is not part of life! That's just mortician philosophy. Everyone else knows when life stops, death begins; it's not part of anything. Whatever you do, Alec, whatever happens, whether you ever see me again after today or not, you have to promise me, get out of that rotten business! You're too cute to spend your life with dead people!

ALEC. I can't quit.

ALISON. Yes, you can!

ALEC. It's not as easy as you think.

ALISON. Everything is easy, Alec, everything! Look at me— I'm pregnant, and the love of my life, the father of my baby, is in Vietnam— I look like a tank—my Aunt Cindy is setting me up with morticians—my life is a mess! But I'm not crushed, you know? I'm not destroyed! Everybody thinks I oughta be, but I'm not! And you know why? Because there's still a bunch of stuff I want to do with my life!

ALEC. Like what?

ALISON. God, I don't know,...stop the war!? Feed the poor. Do you know how many children die in this country every year from diseases related to malnutrition? In this country where there's more food than anywhere else on the planet?

ALEC. How many?

ALISON. A lot, it's like...a lot! And, uh... I want to learn a bunch of languages, I want to see the world... I don't know, I just want to make a difference, you know? Isn't there *anything else* you'd rather do with your life? I mean, you don't *like* what you do, do you?

ALEC. Of course not.

ALISON. Then isn't there something you'd rather do?

ALEC. Sure, there is.

ALISON. What?

ALEC. It's kind of dumb.

ALISON. Just tell me.

ALEC. It's not like "change the world" or anything—

ALISON. Just say it!

ALEC. Well...I always look through the Minneapolis paper on Sundays. And there are always a few small farms for sale outside of the Twin Cities—and it's kind of dumb, but I sometimes, every now and then, think I should check into—maybe—

ALISON. Starting a farm?

ALEC. No, not a farm farm. I don't like cows, they make me kind of uneasy. But I was thinking someday I might want to try and grow...flowers?

ALISON. Flowers?

ALEC. Yeah.

ALISON. But that sounds wonderful, Alec, that doesn't sound dumb!

ALEC. No?

ALISON. No!

ALEC. It's NOT, really, it makes, it kind of makes sense, because all these years of buying flowers for funerals, I've learned a lot about flowers, right? And my mom, when I was little, she gave me all the Audubon guidebooks, and we'd read them before I went to bed, so I know all the wildflowers and the butterflies and everything, so I'm thinking maybe someday—don't ever tell anyone this—I'll sell the business and take that money along with all the money I've saved all these years I haven't had dates?—and maybe buy a farm and grow some wildflowers that I could sell to florists in the Cities and then maybe have a life? *(He pulls a piece of paper from his pocket.)* I saw one in the paper this morning, actually, I cut it out. See? It's in Farmington. Twenty acres. *(A brief pause as he gazes at the paper.)* People in the Cities, I don't think they know... *(And then at ALISON.)* ...how beautiful wildflowers are. *(A moment and then he folds up the paper, pockets it.)* So, someday, you know, that's my master plan, it's sort of dumb—

ALISON. No, you have to do that. You have to. Do it today!

ALEC. I can't do it today.

ALISON. Then do it tomorrow! And if you can't do it tomorrow, then do it today, because you have to do that!

ALEC. Alison, is everyone in Connecticut like you?

ALISON. No! Nobody's like me. Alec, what if I told you I'd marry you right now if you quit?

ALEC. But you won't.

ALISON. What if I did?

ALEC. What about Jerry?

ALISON. Forget about Jerry! What if I told you I'd marry you right now if you quit?

ALEC. I'd quit.

ALISON. There you go! When you find the right girl, you'll quit! See, maybe I should go into politics. *(She stops suddenly, touches her stomach.)* Oh wow.

ALEC. Are you OK?

ALISON. You want to feel something wild?

ALEC. I don't know.

ALISON. Give me your hand. Give. Here. *(ALISON takes his hand and places it low on her abdomen, searching for the baby.)* You're shaking, Alec, you know that?

ALEC. Yeah.

ALISON. There. You feel that?

ALEC. I think.

ALISON. That's a hand. A tiny little hand. Do you feel it?

ALEC. Yeah. Now I do. *(Brief pause.)* Alison?

ALISON. What?

ALEC. What if I think I HAVE found the right girl?

ALISON. You haven't, Alec.

ALEC. What if I think I have?

ALISON. You'd be wrong.

ALEC *(pulling a ring out of his pocket)*. No, I'd be wrong to listen to YOU is how I'd be wrong, if that's how I really felt, right?

ALISON. Alec, is that a ring? *(He descends on one knee.)* Oh, God. Please, Alec, don't get down on one knee!

ALEC. Alison...

ALISON. Alec, I thought we had an understanding, we're friends, we're lonely, get up!

ALEC *(plowing ahead)*. Alison, you're a beautiful woman and you're full of life, in more ways than one. And if you would just be my wife, I promise you I will quit being a mortician right now— I'll raise your kid and teach her how to skate and play hockey on the lake— and in the spring I'll take her out in the fields and show her the goldenrods and the evening primrose and the chicory and the butter-and-eggs and all the little purple prairie flowers—we'll go fishing together and we'll build our own house, and I'll love you and your baby like there's no tomorrow...forever. What do you say?

ALISON. What about Jerry?

ALEC. Forget about Jerry! What do you say?

ALISON. I say, WHAT ABOUT JERRY?

ALEC *(standing up suddenly)*. Jerry's not coming, Alison!

ALISON. What do you mean, "Jerry's not coming"?

ALEC. I mean I'm sorry you made a mistake and trusted the wrong guy—

ALISON. You don't even know Jerry, Alec, how can you talk like this about him? Jerry is a wonderful human being, he's not "a mistake"! He's a gentleman!

ALEC. He knocks you up and disappears and HE'S—?

ALISON. "Knocks me up"?

ALEC. Yes, and then he disappears—

ALISON. "Knocks me UP"?

ALEC. Yes, and HE'S a gentleman?

ALISON. I don't believe you just said that, Alec, "knocks me up"!

ALEC. I don't care, just tell me, if HE can do that and he's a gentleman, then what am I, clanking around out here, what am I?

ALISON. Well, YOU were a gentleman too, until a minute ago when you asked me to marry you and said "knocks me up"! Alec, I'm sorry, you're very sweet, but you don't even know me!

ALEC. I know enough from what your Aunt Cindy—

ALISON. But my Aunt Cindy's a liar! She just wants to make sure I have to live the same tired old dream SHE'S stuck with! I thought you understood that!

ALEC. I do!

ALISON. No, you don't! You don't understand anything! If you did you wouldn't tell me I made a mistake falling in love with Jerry! That's so stupid! No one makes a mistake when they fall in love!

ALEC. That's not true!

ALISON. Yes, it is!

ALEC. No, it's not, because I made a mistake when I fell in love with you.

ALISON. Oh, Alec, you never fell in love with me.

ALEC. Yes, I did!

ALISON. When? When you saw me at some wedding— from a mile away? That's not love.

ALEC. No, not at the wedding! About ten minutes ago— when you said you had more hope and imagination than the whole ugly world! That's when I fell in love with you. But see, it was just a mistake, because you don't even have enough imagination to let go of your hopeless dream about Jerry and live the REAL life you could have right now with me! I know I'm not perfect, but I just said I would give up everything that's real to me just for the chance to be with you, and you, you won't even give up a LIE!

ALISON. Jerry loves me!

ALEC. So where is he?

ALISON. He's coming!

ALEC. When?

ALISON. I don't know! But does that mean I'm wrong? Just because I don't know? It doesn't mean I'm wrong!

(She starts to cry. Brief pause. ALEC awkwardly embraces her. After a moment, they kiss. They separate for a moment. In the distance, the train goes by. Then AL-

ISON surprises ALEC by kissing him again, more passionately this time. When they separate from the long kiss, both are heart-poundingly befuddled. CINDY enters.)

CINDY. Baby? *(ALEC and ALISON move apart from each other.)* Guess what?
ALISON. What?
CINDY. Jerry's here.

(Music suddenly rises and JERRY, a very handsome man in a Coast Guard uniform, appears alone in a circle of light. Nearby is a camera on tripod with an air-pump remote control. He sings.)

JERRY.
> BE MY LOVE, FOR NO ONE ELSE CAN END THIS YEARNING,
> THIS NEED THAT YOU AND YOU ALONE CREATE.
> JUST FILL MY ARMS THE WAY YOU'VE FILLED MY DREAMS.
> THE DREAMS THAT YOU INSPIRE WITH EVERY SWEET DESIRE.
> BE MY LOVE, AND WITH YOUR KISSES SET ME BURNING.
> ONE KISS IS ALL I NEED TO SEAL MY FATE.
> AND HAND IN HAND, WE'LL FIND LOVE'S PROMISED LAND.
> THERE'LL BE NO ONE BUT YOU FOR ME ETERNALLY
> IF YOU WOULD BE MY LOVE.

(As he finishes singing, the lights rise to reveal ALISON, CINDY, LINDY, and ALEC.)

JERRY. Alison Farnham, I have seen the whole world. I've literally sailed the Seven Seas. And nothing on God's green Earth is as dear to me or starts a fire in my heart faster than the sight of your sweet little face. The months we've been apart have been the hardest months of my life. I don't ever want to be separated from you again. I love you, I need you, and I want you to marry me. Will you marry me? *(He has pulled a ring from his pocket and is presenting it to ALISON.)*

ALISON. Yes.

JERRY. Then I am the happiest man that lives. *(He slips the ring on her finger and kisses her. JERRY pulls away, picks an apple, and hands it to ALISON.)*

ALISON. How did you find me?

JERRY. I called your mom and she told me where you were.

ALISON. Did she tell you about the baby?

JERRY *(as in "Holy Shit, she nearly bit my ear off through the phone")*. She certainly did.

ALISON. And she didn't call me?

JERRY. She was gonna, but I begged her to let it be a surprise. Surprised?

ALISON. Yes! So you came back for ME?

JERRY *(a little confused by the question)*. I did!

ALISON. Not for the baby.

JERRY *(still a little confused)*. That's right.

ALISON. Then I'm the happiest girl that lives!

JERRY *("Who cares? Women are just plain confusing!")*. Capital! *(They kiss. JERRY stands her in front of the camera, then turns to LINDY.)* Lindy? Sir, can I call you Lindy? I understand you like to be called Lindy?

LINDY. That's my name, Jerry, don't wear it out.

JERRY. Lindy, I've got an idea about these apples of yours I'd like to share with you over a great big dinner down at Sundberg's Cafe?

LINDY. You're just in time, tonight's supposed to be the first frost. What's the idea?

JERRY. I'll tell you two words.

LINDY. Go ahead.

JERRY. Outer. Space.

LINDY. Outer. Space.

JERRY. Outer space. Don't say no!

LINDY. I'm not. But I do want you to know, Jerry, how glad I am you came through for Alison.

JERRY. Sir, the pleasure's all mine. Annnd, we'll put you right here. Perfect. Good-looking man, you musta had lot of girl trouble.

LINDY. Still do, Jerry. Still do. *(JERRY hands LINDY an apple and stands him in front of the camera, then goes to CINDY.)*

JERRY. Now, ma'am, I can see you've got it in for me, and I'll tell you what, that's perfectly understandable. I should never have let serving my country come between me and your niece, whose love for me is gonna outlive this nation and every other earthly empire. In fact, if I hadn't gotten shot in the leg like I did about two months ago— *(To ALISON.)* Don't worry, darlin', I'm fine— *(To CINDY.)* I would have been back a hell of a lot sooner, but that's neither here nor there. What matters is, you and I are going to be having Christmas dinner together for the next forty years, so what do you say, benefit of the doubt? I showed up!

CINDY. How about we wait and see?

JERRY. Capital! Annnnd, we'll slide you right over here ... unless, of course, you want to be next to your sweetheart.

CINDY. No, I'm fine right where I am.

JERRY. Far be it from me. *(JERRY kisses CINDY on the cheek and hands her an apple. Then he goes to ALEC.)* Alec!

ALEC. What?

JERRY. Alec. Cindy's explained to me here, very hush-hush, about you, and I think, what a thing to do to come calling on my little firecracker when she's already pregnant with MY baby? MY little munchkin!

ALEC. You're mad.

JERRY. No! Heck no! Why would I be mad? Everybody nowadays wants to know where the real men are? The ones who fight for what's right? Who go out on a limb when a girl's in distress? I'll tell you where they are, they're not just in Vietnam holding up the dominoes, they're right here. They're standing right in front of me. They're YOU. You're a damn hero, Alec Willoughby, and a gentleman to boot! Thanks for looking out for my girl. *(He embraces ALEC, then steps away.)*

ALEC *(uncomfortably)*. Anytime.

JERRY. You want to be in the picture?

ALEC. I don't think so.

JERRY. Alec!

ALEC. I don't think I should.

JERRY. Don't let bitterness eat your heart out, Alec. What a plague. You loved her ten minutes ago—I'm here now—I'm sorry—do the right thing! Be in the picture!

ALEC. Jerry, you're right.

JERRY. I am. You're right!

ALEC. But I can't do it.

JERRY. Alec! Don't be a turd in the punchbowl, you're breaking my stride! Be in the picture!

ALEC. I'm sorry, Jerry. Alison?

JERRY. Wait a minute, I'm taking a picture here!

ALISON. It's OK, Jerry, the picture can wait a second, I think? *(ALISON takes ALEC aside.)* What is it?

ALEC. Listen, I'll be in the picture if you really want me to, but—

ALISON. It's all right, Alec, you don't have to.

ALEC. See, I want to be in the picture for you if you want me to be in it, that's all. But only if you want me to be in it.

ALISON. Then be in the picture.

ALEC. I'll be in the picture.

ALISON. Good.

JERRY. Capital! Let's put you right here, Alec, right on the other side of the bride-to-be. *(JERRY hands ALEC an apple and then goes behind the camera and sets the timer. Meticulously:)* By the way...I don't know if any of you have caught on to this yet...but I do not know a thing about taking photographs. I just bought this darn piece of machinery in Minneapolis yesterday afternoon because I had a sneaking suspicion today might be momentous. So. I know this is a strange situation for all of us, but personally, I try not to let reality confuse things

any more than they already are. *(JERRY plucks an apple from a tree and takes his position in the picture.)*
ALISON. Jerry, let's never be apart again, OK?
JERRY. Aw, wouldn't that be nice? Unfortunately, darlin', I gotta be back in Vietnam in nine days. Smile! *(JERRY tosses his apple into the air, there's an unnaturally bright flash, like a firework, which falls away into snowy, sparkling stardust as music rises and the stage fades quickly to black.)*

END OF ACT ONE

ACT TWO

AT RISE: *The next day. Lights come up on JERRY, LINDY and ALISON in the orchard on a chilly bright morning. LINDY and JERRY are carefully picking apples from bushel baskets and dropping them in a bucket of water, then meticulously drying them off, shining them up, and wrapping them carefully in crumpled newspaper and packing them into a cardboard box.*

JERRY. I'm no rocket scientist, Lindy, but I got a funny feeling you send these apples of yours to my buddy Etch at NASA, and all your problems are gonna be solved.
LINDY *(skeptical, amused)*. Jerry, do you actually know for a fact they're looking for apples?
JERRY. They're lookin' for everything! Lindy, this is a tremendous endeavor they're undertaking, putting a man on the moon, you don't know! My buddy Etch told me they've got dietitians, fuel chemists, sonar guys, electronic computer geniuses, wizards of gravity particles, even *theologians*—the public doesn't know about *that*, of course, because of national security, but every single angle of this moonshot is being very carefully examined. I mean, what *if* God's up there? Right? Or Martians? Did you ever think about that? Our guys're gonna need food—!—to keep up the strength with the negotiations! And what if it turns out they can't come back, for tech-

48

nological reasons? What if the moon moves—it happened once!—they're taking years of supplies! It's like down at Cape Kennedy right now, they're building a whole new world, Lindy, just for insurance purposes, you know, just to *bring along in case*, and maybe, I can't promise anything, but maybe they can start theirs like we did this one, with a sweet little apple! You never know!

LINDY. Jerry, there's not many times in my life I've felt like saying this to another man...but I want you to know...I really like you. You're something else.

ALISON *(pouty)*. He certainly is, isn't he.

JERRY *(with a sidewise look at ALISON)*. All I am, Lindy—and thank you, but it's something anybody can be—is excited about Life. Every morning I wake up, I don't know about you, but I thank God. A lot of people bitch and moan, they've got problems— I don't get it! Because if the sun is up and there's air for me to breathe, then I've got a project and get outta my way! Which reminds me. *(He pulls out a piece of paper and hands it to LINDY, then continues working.)*

LINDY. What's this?

JERRY. Well, I took the liberty of writing this note explaining your situation, about having all these apples slapped in your lap by a profusion of nature, etcetera, and I quoted a price for 'em I think everyone will agree is high but fair. And I also tried my best, even though I'm no apple-scientist—what the word for that would be, I don't know—I tried to make 'em sound like they would be especially good for use in outer space.

ALISON. Jerry, that is the stupidest thing I've ever heard in my life. What could possibly make an apple "especially good for use in outer space"?

JERRY *(after a beat, caught off guard)*. Well, darlin', that's the puzzle, isn't it... but I put it very poetically, and they got a ton of money right now and they're casting about for ideas, so, we'll see, won't we, what's the matter with YOU?

ALISON. Oh, like you care.

JERRY. Darlin', of course I care, what kind of thing is that to say... *(Turning away from her to LINDY.)* Lindy, you want to sign right there. Oops, wait a minute!

LINDY. What?

JERRY. You don't have any relatives in the federal government of the United States, do you?

LINDY. Not that I know of.

JERRY. OK, because, just so you know, all offers null and void upon a revelation like that, anyway, sign here. *(Turning to ALISON.)* Now, what's the matter, darlin'?

LINDY *(signs)*. Here you go.

JERRY. I'll take that letter.

ALISON *(dejected)*. Nothing.

JERRY *(to LINDY)*. Capital! That's a real John Hancock you got there, Lindy.

LINDY. I figure they oughta know who they're dealing with.

JERRY. Damn straight! —Darn straight, excuse me. *(JERRY pockets the letter and continues packing apples.)* I try not to use too much uncouth toilet talk around the little lady here, but being in the service, what a tough habit to break. You ever in?

LINDY. World War II, First Infantry.

JERRY. Ouch! Big Red! I personally haven't seen any combat yet but I'm thinking I will very soon.

LINDY. Why do you say that?

JERRY. Well, nobody knows this, Lindy, so "loose lips sink ships," but a buddy of mine in II Corps says pretty soon there's gonna be a big authorization—a hundred thousand new troops—and we're gonna end this little conflagration once and for all. That's the plan anyway.

LINDY. Let's hope it works.

JERRY. I'm pretty sure it will, I mean, I'm no General Westmoreland, but I don't see a *lot* that could go wrong—

ALISON. Jerry?

JERRY. What, darlin'?

ALISON. Don't go back.

JERRY *(amused, to LINDY)*. You hear that, Lindy? "Don't go back"...isn't that sweet? That's like a movie.

ALISON. Jerry, you're gonna get killed!

JERRY. No, I'm not! Look, darlin', I *gotta* be in Honolulu a week from tomorrow to get that ship to Da Nang, and that's just the way it is. Now my hitch is up in three years, and won't that be great, but you and Junior are just gonna have to bear with me 'til then. OK? OK? *(JERRY closes the box and begins methodically taping it shut.)*

ALISON. Maybe...

JERRY *(a little frustrated)*. Maybe what?

ALISON *(getting upset)*. Maybe...this is all just really...a mistake.

JERRY. No, it's not, it's just hard, that's all.

LINDY *(backing away)*. I'm gonna leave you two to—

ALISON. Uncle Lindy, you stay right there! This is not going to take very long!

JERRY. Your mom understood, darlin', she was happy that I just showed up! She figures you'll live with her until...

ALISON. But I don't want to live with my mother! Yuck! What happened, did you two sit around the coffee table and plan out my life for me?

JERRY. I'm just trying to do the right thing here—

ALISON. I want us to have our *own* house, Jerry, with a yard for the baby to play in—

JERRY. And we'll have that—

ALISON. I don't believe you're going back, this is so stupid!

JERRY. I know it is, darlin', but I don't know what you were thinking it was gonna be like, either!

ALISON. I thought it was gonna be like how you SAID it would be, you jerk! I thought we'd be together! I didn't think you'd be going off to fight in stupid Vietnam!

JERRY. Look, *I have to go*, Alison, I owe them the time, don't do this to me!

ALISON. Do this to *me*? You owe *them*? Do you listen to yourself when you talk, do you even hear what you're saying? Look at me, Jerry, this is your baby, where the hell have you BEEN?

JERRY. I didn't know!

ALISON. I KNOW you didn't know, but you didn't write either! And that's not right!

LINDY. Really, I could...go.

ALISON *(to LINDY)*. No! Stay! I want you to know what your friend here is doing to me!

JERRY. Doing to YOU?

ALISON. By making me get married!

JERRY. Darlin', we *gotta* get married!

ALISON. What's the point, though, if you're not even going to *be here*?

JERRY. "What's the point"? We got Junior on the way!

ALISON. That doesn't change anything!

JERRY. What the hell are you talking about? You can't have a baby without a husband!
ALISON. But don't you see, that's exactly what I'm getting! *(She starts pulling off her ring.)*
JERRY. What the hell are you doing?
ALISON. I don't want to have a big wedding just to say goodbye, Jerry, that'll be so stupid!
JERRY. Now wait a minute...
ALISON. It would!
JERRY. Darlin', you're not really saying you don't want to get married, are you?
ALISON. I love you more than anything, Jerry, but really, what's the point?! *(She gives the ring to JERRY and exits crying into the house. Long pause. JERRY, having finished taping the box, addresses LINDY.)*
JERRY. Lindy, these little sonsabitches are good to go. My buddy Etch'll take a look at 'em—you figure you got two weeks?
LINDY. Maybe three. They can freeze-in a good quarter-inch and still be all right. After that, though, it's gonna be over.
JERRY *(picks up the ring)*. You ever seen a woman like that in your life?
LINDY. Every day. Every single day.
JERRY. You don't think she's serious, do you? About calling off the wedding?
LINDY. I think she's serious *now*. But that doesn't mean she won't seriously change her mind a little bit later, either, you know women.
JERRY. Lindy, you were in the service, you know as well as I do I can't—
LINDY. Jerry, look—

JERRY. I'm trying my best—
LINDY. Jerry, look, don't worry about it. It's girl stuff, she'll come around.
JERRY. You think so?
LINDY. I know so. But, Jerry, listen. What *I* would take away from all this, if I were you, is: when you go back to Vietnam... *write her back.*
JERRY *(like a prizefighter)*. Write her back.
LINDY. Write her back. OK?
JERRY. Yes sir. *(JERRY picks up the box of apples.)*
LINDY. Hey, tell me something, have you seen *Spartacus*?
JERRY. Are you kidding? Three times!
LINDY. Wasn't that something? What was Tony Curtis up to in that picture you think?
JERRY. I don't know, I didn't much care for that either. *(Door slams.)*
LINDY. Oh shit, here comes trouble.

(CINDY enters.)

CINDY *(amiable but efficient)*. There's some apple pie cooling on the windowsill, Jerry, if you want a piece.
JERRY *(vaguely solicitous)*. Thank you, ma'am. Maybe when we get back from town. *(LINDY and JERRY start to go.)*
CINDY *(hard and fast)*. Lindy!
LINDY *(to JERRY)*. I'll meet you at the car in a second, Jerry.
JERRY. Capital. *(JERRY exits.)*
CINDY *(sotto voce at first)*. Would you like to tell me, sir, what the H-E-double toothpicks is going on around here? That girl just ran by me in tears? What on earth did you DO?

LINDY. I didn't do anything, what are you—
CINDY. So what just happened?
LINDY. Nothing!
CINDY. Lindy! *(Brief pause.)*
LINDY. They had a little fight, that's all.
CINDY. A little fight.
LINDY. Yes!
CINDY. About what?
LINDY. I'm not gonna tell you about what, it'll only start you meddling again! Haven't you caused enough trouble as it is, dragging that mortician into things? Jesus, go bake a cake or something and stay out of other people's business! *(LINDY tries to evade her, but she stops him.)*
CINDY. Where do you think you're going?
LINDY. I'm going to mail my apples to NASA, would you stop barking at me?
CINDY. You're not really!
LINDY. I am too really, I'm on government business, so step aside!
CINDY. Lindy, this has got to be the most lamebrained scheme I have ever heard tell of. You don't honestly think they're going to buy YOUR apples, do you?
LINDY. Cindy—
CINDY. For the MOON?
LINDY. I don't know! But it's an interesting idea, Cindy, and it beats the hell out of applesauce for keeping me occupied and you outta my hair! Jesus, is somebody paying you to aggravate me? They're getting their money's worth!*(Just as he's about to exit, she obstructs his path.)*
CINDY. Look, you're gonna tell me what happened eventually, mister, you might as well tell me now.

LINDY. You know, you think you know me, Cindy, but you don't.

CINDY. Oh, I do too know you—

LINDY. No, you know your own little twisted idea of me and that's about it! *(Tapping his head.)* I got all kinds of secrets in here!

CINDY. What just happened?

LINDY. I'm having three different affairs right now, Cindy, right under your nose, did you know *that*?

CINDY. What just happened?

LINDY. Three different women, all young, all different colors!

CINDY. Lindy, I'll find out! You know I will! Just tell me now!

LINDY. I'm not talking to you anyway, don't you remember?

CINDY. Tell me now! *(Brief pause.)* Tell me now! *(Long pause.)* Tell me now!

LINDY *(quickly and quietly)*. She said the wedding's off.

CINDY. Oh Jesus, Mary, and Joseph!

LINDY. It's not a big deal.

CINDY. Lindy, we have Pastor Ed coming out here Saturday for a wedding! This is a big deal!

LINDY. Cindy, it's not a big deal because you'll talk to her!

CINDY. Oh, *I'll* talk to her?

LINDY. Of course you will!

CINDY. So I guess I AM good for something around here, huh?

LINDY. Well, considering you never shut up, we might as well take advantage of it.

CINDY. You know, I have wanted a divorce ever since we got married!

LINDY. Yeah? I've wanted one ever since we MET!

(LINDY exits. CINDY exits into the house. Lights shift. Time passes. ALISON enters, reading a letter to herself.)

ALISON. Dear Alec. It's me. Alison. Wondering where you are, and how you're doing. I know you probably don't ever want to hear from me again, after everything I put you through yesterday. But I wanted to make sure you knew how much our short time together meant. To me, at least. I feel like yesterday the train of my life stopped for a moment in a totally new and beautiful, pure and peaceful place, you know? And out the window in the sun was you, and your dream of a field full of flowers, and the way time seemed to stand still while we were together—it was all just out the window there. But today I woke up, Alec, and I don't know about you, but I am like a million miles past that place. Now it feels like I'm at the edge of a big frozen wasteland, and I think this is where they're gonna make me live. Alec, our time together was so short...but I know I will miss you forever. Goodbye. Sincerely, Alison. P.S. I love you. Ha ha.

(She folds the letter, kisses it, slips it an envelope and seals it. CINDY enters.)

CINDY. Baby, what on earth are you doing out here?

ALISON. Nothing.

CINDY. You're liable to catch your death, come on back in the house. *(ALISON doesn't move.)* Come on back in the house now. I found Heather's wedding dress, I need you to try it on so I can let it out.

ALISON. No matter how much you let it out, I'm gonna look like a big jelly doughnut.

CINDY. No, you won't.

ALISON. I'm not getting married anyway.

CINDY *(after a beat)*. So I heard. You want to talk about it?

ALISON. No.

CINDY. OK. *(Brief pause.)* Who's that letter to?

ALISON. Alec.

CINDY. Alec? What about?

ALISON. Nothing. Just about...how much I miss him...

CINDY *(slightly horrified)*. Baby, that's not right.

ALISON. But—

CINDY. No, it's not right, give me that letter.

ALISON. No.

CINDY. You give it to me now.

ALISON. I will not!

CINDY. Ali, that baby inside you is Jerry's, not Alec's, there is no getting around that. Now give me that letter!

ALISON. But Jerry's not making me happy!

CINDY. I know that, but—

ALISON. He's going back to Vietnam, and he won't even be here a week, and he's being so mean, it's all so stupid!

CINDY. Oh, baby... *(CINDY takes ALISON in her arms.)*

ALISON. Could he even just come out for dinner?

CINDY. Who, Alec?

ALISON. Yeah?

CINDY. Of course not!

ALISON. —or something?—

CINDY. Ali—

ALISON. Why is that such a bad idea?

CINDY. Because, Ali! Letting Alec be in the picture yesterday was one thing, OK? But to have him—hanging around...while you and Jerry are trying to start a life...

ALISON. It'd just be dinner, though, wouldn't it?

CINDY. But don't you see how having him over for dinner after all that might be a little bit of an...insult?

ALISON *(actually confused)*. Kind of, I guess.

CINDY. It's a dignity thing.

ALISON. For guys.

CINDY. For anybody, baby!

ALISON. But if Alec's really in love with me, and Jerry's really in love with me, then shouldn't they at least be able to be friends?

CINDY. That's not the way it works, though, baby. When two men want the same woman, that's what they call "bad."

ALISON. Usually! But what if—

CINDY. No!

ALISON. But—

CINDY *(firm)*. No. And that's all there is to it. Now you and I are going to go back into the house and try on that wedding dress, and when Jerry gets back from town I want you tell him you know life isn't perfect but you love him and you think he's gonna be a wonderful daddy.

ALISON. Why...why do I have to do that?

CINDY. Because, Ali, you two went and made a baby. It's that simple. You made a baby. And the both of you owe it to that baby now to try and make this work.

ALISON. So you're saying I have no choice.

CINDY. I'm so sorry, Alison, but I am. This baby is real. You have to get married to Jerry. I wish it could be another way, you know I do, I wish it so much I could just break in two, *but it can't*. This is just the way life IS.

(LINDY has just entered with JERRY, who is carrying a few shopping bags.)

JERRY. Hey, darlin'. *(ALISON does not respond.)*

CINDY. Hi, Jerry. *(To ALISON.)* When you're ready to come in, you come in. *(To JERRY.)* Don't keep her out here too long. It's getting cold. *(CINDY walks sullenly past LINDY and into the house. LINDY doggedly follows. JERRY and ALISON sit on the steps.)*

JERRY. Your Uncle Lindy showed me around town some.

ALISON. Yeah?

JERRY. I don't think I've ever seen so many bars on one block.

ALISON. There's not much to do out here but drink, I guess. And fight.

JERRY. I got you some things.

ALISON. Oh, you didn't have to do that.

JERRY. Sure I did. Here, darlin'. Take a look. *(JERRY pulls a box out of one of the bags.)*

ALISON. What's that, a cake?

JERRY. Yeah. And I got it inscribed, look. Check that out. *(JERRY opens the top of the box and shows it to her.)*

ALISON *(reading the cake).* "Yes sir, that's my baby."

JERRY. And they do that for free, too! I always thought that was extra. That's not all, though, darlin', look at this. *(From another bag, he pulls out a large box. He hands it to ALISON.)* What do you think of that?

ALISON. A train set.

JERRY. For Junior. I always wanted one when I was a kid, so I figured, you know, here's my chance. And there's a whole little town that goes with it, too, darlin', with people and trees, there's even a little Howard Johnson's, like the one we had breakfast at in Groton, remember, that morning? Anyway, here's the grand finale. *(JERRY pulls from another bag a large denim maternity jumper with a huge apple on the front with a bite taken out of it. He holds it up to himself.)* Isn't it perfect? *(Brief pause.)*

ALISON. Uhh—

JERRY. It's not for me.

ALISON. I know, Jerry.

JERRY. I saw it in the window and it was like, ding! You like it?

ALISON. It's nice.

JERRY. It's perfect, isn't it, I mean, with the apples and you and the whole thing. Can't go wrong. What's the matter, darlin'? Are you crying?

ALISON. No.

JERRY. Hey. *(He takes her in his arms.)* Can I tell you something?

ALISON. What?

JERRY. I was thinking in town, you know: I'm brave about everything but you.

ALISON. Yeah?

JERRY. Yeah. I had a whole ship run over me once when I was working in a buoy cage in the Marshall Islands, and I wasn't half as scared then, bouncing and clanking around underneath that ship as I am whenever I get around you. And, darlin', believe me, I know exactly what you mean about me being gone all the time, I know it's not a good way to be married. My dad was a Coastie and he was never around, and when my mom died, I had to keep her casket in the house for two weeks waiting for him to get clearance to come home and see her. So I know it's not ideal. I do. But, darlin', I gotta be honest with you. When I die, and my mind flips back through the pages, trying to find what really mattered? If I had to pick which moments to look at right before I slipped away, I know every one of those moments would be on a ship in the middle of the ocean, because that's the only place my soul is really satisfied. I mean, I can talk a good game back here in polite society, and I do like a pretty girl—well, one pretty girl in particular—but at heart?—I'm a sailor. And like my daddy used to say to me, "Sailors belong on ships and ships belong at sea." And it's true. I love you SO much, darlin'...but I don't know what I'd become if I left the service—probably some sort of monster. And that wouldn't be good for you or Junior.

ALISON. But it won't be good for us if you get killed, either.

JERRY. Darlin', I won't get killed. I promise. Look, you want this war to end? Let me go. Send me back. Let me do my job and I guarantee you in six months time there won't be one American soldier left over there. Westmoreland and all those fellas in the big-pants club, they got it all worked out. And I'll come home in three years to you and Junior and we'll be stationed in Groton or San Francisco or who knows where—

ALISON *(cutting in a little enthusiastically)*. I'd like to go to San Francisco.

JERRY. Then that's where we'll go! That's exactly where we'll go! Just tell me when I come home that you and Junior'll be waiting. It's just three years away, darlin'. Every kind of happiness you ever dreamed of us having is just three years away. Can't you hold on 'til then? Please? I love you so much. Please? *(Brief pause. JERRY takes out his ring and holds it out to her. After a moment, she takes it and puts it on.)*

ALISON. I guess so.

(They kiss. LINDY enters.)

LINDY. Jerry? Alison?
ALISON. Yeah? *(Brief pause.)*
LINDY. Alec's here.

(Lights shift. ALEC appears in a small circle of light, playing a guitar and singing. Near him is a bright orange box.)

ALEC.
>COME GATHER 'ROUND, PEOPLE, WHEREVER YOU ROAM.
>AND ADMIT THAT THE WATERS AROUND YOU HAVE GROWN.
>AND FACE IT, THAT SOON, YOU'LL BE DRENCHED TO THE BONE.
>IF YOUR TIME TO YOU IS WORTH SAVING,
>THEN YOU BETTER START SWIMMING
>OR YOU'LL SINK LIKE A STONE,
>'CAUSE THE TIMES, THEY ARE A-CHANGIN'.

(Lights rise revealing JERRY, ALISON, CINDY, and LINDY all gathered around. ALEC goes to ALISON.)

ALEC. Alison, I went down to Farmington this morning. Like you said. And I met this fella, he teaches Romantic Literature at Carleton College down there in Northfield, and his wife's from Argentina—can you believe that? And they said if I wanted I could lease the place from 'em. For a year or two to start with? So—I did! And I'm moving down there week after next. They've got horses, and a few goats, and a real nice piece of land. And this fella, he makes his own beer that he let me try? And you know, it was good! Anyway, uh, you know how I feel, I don't need to say it in front of all these people, do I? *(ALEC pulls out a ring and puts it in ALISON's hand.)*

JERRY *(to ALEC)*. You little son of a bitch—

ALISON. Jerry!

JERRY. I'm gonna stomp a mudhole in your ass that'll make Lake Ponchartrain look like a finger bowl!

ALISON. Jerry—

JERRY. You ready?

CINDY. Lindy, do something!

LINDY *(deadpan)*. Please, Jerry, stop, don't. *(JERRY starts pushing ALEC around.)*

ALEC. Listen, fella ... you're not the boss of me!

CINDY. Lindy!

JERRY. That's MY baby, pal, not yours!

ALISON *(outraged)*. YOUR baby?

JERRY. Damn straight!

ALEC. Yeah? No one would know it was yours from the way you—

JERRY. The way I what?

ALEC. The way you—

JERRY. What?

ALEC. Knocked her up!

ALISON. "Knocked me UP"?

ALEC. And then disappeared and never wrote back!

ALISON. "Knocked me UP"! *(To ALEC.)* Why do you say that, "knocked me up"?! You're lucky I don't knock YOU up!

JERRY. I'll tell you one thing, pal, I'm not sorry for anything I've done!

ALEC. Yeah, well everybody else is!

JERRY. That does it! *(JERRY punches ALEC hard in the stomach, and he falls to the ground.)*

CINDY. Jerry, stop it!

JERRY *(to CINDY)*. Mrs. Linda, you stay the hell out of this!

ALISON. Jerry!

JERRY. And you too! This is all your fault anyway, you two-timing—

ALISON. What?

JERRY. Nothing!

ALISON. Two-timing WHAT?

CINDY. Young man, that mouth of yours is gonna get you in serious trouble!

JERRY. I'm already in serious trouble! I come back from VIETNAM...

ALISON. Oh, give me a break!

JERRY. ...from *defending my country*...

ALISON. Nobody asked you to come back!

JERRY. The shit they didn't!

CINDY *(shrill)*. Mouth!

JERRY. I got a goddamn letter every day—

CINDY *(shrill)*. Mouth!

JERRY. Mrs. Linda, please, would you shut the fuck up!? *(CINDY is outraged beyond belief. LINDY is laughing. ALEC, meanwhile, has recovered. To ALISON:)* I got a letter every day, saying, "When are you coming back? When are you coming back?"

ALEC. So THIS is a gentleman? THIS is a "wonderful human being"?

ALISON *(confused)*. Well, I thought he was once, I don't know...

JERRY. And when I DO come back, what do I find but MY GIRL two-timing me with a creepy little mortician!

ALISON. Well what else was I supposed to do, you never wrote back!

JERRY. I told you, I got shot in the leg!

ALISON. Oh, and do you write with your leg? Do you dial a phone with your leg?

ALEC *(to ALISON)*. You must think I'm really pathetic.

ALISON. Alec, please, you're freaking me out! *(To JERRY.)* I'M stuck with this baby no matter what, but you think YOU'RE a big hero, just because you "showed up"! Well is that all you have to do now to be a man is SHOW UP? Just SHOW UP? *I don't think so!*

JERRY. I don't think so either!

ALEC *(to ALISON)*. You must think I'm not even worth the time of day, to say no to me for THIS LUNKHEAD!

JERRY. Lunkhead?

ALISON. Alec—

ALEC. No, don't talk to me! Don't talk to me ever again! *(To JERRY.)* She's all yours, take her, you two morons deserve each other!

JERRY. Moron?

ALEC *(to ALISON)*. I never loved you anyway, I was just... *(Seeing ALISON is hurt, he slows down.)* I was just being noble...

ALISON. This is NOT...I repeat, NOT...the way...the two of you...you're impossible! I'm...I'm...I'm going home to Mystic! And I never want to see either one of you ever again! *(She throws a ring at each of her suitors and starts to exit.)*

CINDY. Baby, you can't—
ALISON *(almost shrieking).* Don't tell me what I can't do, you crazy old lady, I'll do whatever I want! *(She storms out and, without skipping a beat, CINDY turns on LINDY and starts stalking him around.)*
CINDY *(to LINDY).* Ohhhh, don't think I don't see what YOU'RE doing.
LINDY. Woman, have you gone completely out of your mind?
CINDY. No, you'll ruin everybody's life in the bargain just to make sure you don't get left alone with *me!*
LINDY *(amazed and fumbling).* How could *I*, it was Alec, he showed up, I've got nothing to do with it!
CINDY. No, you do, though, you do!
LINDY. How could I?
CINDY. You didn't send him away, *("and now I'm gonna have to raise that baby!")*
LINDY *(overlapping). ("Cindy, you send them away, they don't leave!")* What am I supposed to do?
CINDY. You're supposed to help me get what I want out of life every now and then, you goon! But you never ever do and that's because you hate me and you hate my dreams!
LINDY. Cindy, for Christ's sake, if you want to open a little knickknack shop, do it, but do you always have to talk like you're painting the goddamn Sistine Chapel?
CINDY. See, you have never respected me or my work.
LINDY. What work?
CINDY. My ART!
LINDY. *Cindy, your art is not so hot! (Brief pause. As CINDY starts to cry, she turns and exits into the house. JERRY and ALEC are watching LINDY. Really mad:)*

What the hell are you looking at? This kind of horseshit happens. It's not a problem. It's just life! It's just goddamn married life! And ONE of you better get used to it!

(LINDY exits into the house. JERRY and ALEC look at each other. All the lights go out. Slowly, the sky fills with the northern lights. They shimmer and undulate while music plays. Then lights slowly rise on ALEC and JERRY. It's later, on a peaceful, very cold, night. ALEC and JERRY watch the lights in the sky as they talk. ALEC still has his orange box with him.)

JERRY. Tell me how you do it.

ALEC. You don't want to know.

JERRY. It's that bad? Tell me how. It's that bad?

ALEC. If you don't know.

JERRY. Just tell me how you do it. A little. Just tell me the barest little, come on. You stick 'em?—you pour what? Something? No, don't tell me, you're right. It's morbid. It's morbid, I shouldn't dwell on it. I'm not as strong as you. You face that truck head-on every day. I'm a mere mortal. I can take it, though, I think, just tell me.

ALEC. I had a body come in with no head once.

JERRY. Ouch! Don't tell me any more. Tell me.

ALEC. I unzipped the bag and there was no head.

JERRY. Ouch! Yikes. Go ahead.

ALEC. It turned out the paramedics had stuffed it down between the guy's legs, so it wouldn't bounce around.

JERRY. Ow! Jesus jumpin' Christ! And you—what?—you sew it? You sewed it? With a big spike or something?—to hold it?

ALEC. It was a closed casket, it didn't matter.

JERRY. OOWWWWCCCH! And how the hell did that happen then? Marital dispute? Domestic crime of some sort?

ALEC. It was a car accident. This fella's Volkswagen had slid under a semi and sheared the top of the car and the fella right off.

JERRY. Ouch! I think I'm getting goose bumps. I'm getting hives! You have seen it all, I bet! You're like a god!

ALEC. No.

JERRY. Oh yeah, you must walk down the street and see everybody with a clock on their chest.

ALEC. Not really.

JERRY. Oh, come on! No head!

ALEC. No head.

JERRY. Ouch! So how do you do it? I can take it. It can't be worse than no head. Just tell me.

ALEC. There's a pump—

JERRY. Oh Joe, don't tell me! Jesus. Tell me.

ALEC. And coming out of the pump is a rubber tube that ends in a thick hollow needle—

JERRY. Yikes! Ouch!

ALEC. They're dead!

JERRY. They're dead.

ALEC. It doesn't hurt.

JERRY. Right, but still! Alec! A big thick metal needle! Hollow!

ALEC. And you cut a vein in the throat and an artery in the leg and you stick the needle into the leg and start the pump.

JERRY. Oh, it makes a bad noise, I bet?

ALEC. It does.

JERRY. Oh, wow, what kind of noise?

ALEC. A bubbling, pumping noise.

JERRY. It would be, wouldn't it?

ALEC. But here's the worst part. You pump the embalming fluid into the body, which is pink—

JERRY. The body is pink?

ALEC. No, the body is grey.

JERRY. I've never seen a dead body. I probably will soon, when I get back to 'Nam, but not yet.

ALEC. They're not pink.

JERRY. OK, I'll know. So what's the worst part?

ALEC. The worst part is, as you pump the embalming fluid into the femoral artery, the old brown blood runs out through the jugular vein and down these gutters in the table, which is tilted—

JERRY. Oh no, it's tilted! I knew, in the picture in my head it was tilted!

ALEC *(with much gravity)*. And the blood just runs down the drain. *(Brief pause.)*

JERRY. Yeah? And?

ALEC. I don't know, to me that's always been the worst part. *(Brief pause.)*

JERRY. Wow! I'm never gonna die now. No way. Yikes. No head!

ALEC. No head.

JERRY. Ouch!

(ALISON enters upstage.)

JERRY *(sotto voce)*. Uh-oh. Ixnay on the oh-nay ed-hay.

ALEC *(sotto voce)*. Got it.

JERRY *(sotto voce)*. Ouch. *(There is a long, uncomfortable pause as ALISON steps between the two men. Finally, they speak.)*

ALISON. Hi.

ALEC. Hi.

JERRY. Hi.

ALISON. Well, I have just been browbeaten by four different people, two of whom *claim* to be my parents—they were on the phone, so I can't be sure—but I think the consensus is I expect too much from life and I need to wise up. So I was thinking we should all just kill ourselves.

JERRY *(actually shocked)*. No, don't even talk like that, darlin', you don't know about the pump!

ALISON. What pump?

ALEC. Jerry!

JERRY. Oh, goddamn it...look: *don't die, not ever.*

ALISON. OK, Jerry, I won't. *(Brief pause.)* So, there's this train that leaves around midnight.

ALEC. The Empire Builder.

ALISON. I guess. Aunt Cindy made the call. That sounds right, though.

ALEC. That's the one that comes through—

ALISON. —yeah—

ALEC. —that time of night—

ALISON. That was it. The Empire Builder. So. I guess I'll be going home. *(They all look up at the sky.)* God, what an unlikely world, huh? Where the sky can be filled with lights like that? We don't have that out East, you know.

ALEC. No?

ALISON. Not really. There's, uh, too many lights, I think. Even when we are that far north. I've got a second cousin in Biddeford Pool, at the School for Osteopathic Medicine, he says he's seen 'em once or twice. But that's it.

JERRY. I saw 'em in Labrador once. I thought it was the end of the world.

ALISON *(a little pouty)*. Maybe it was. *(Brief pause as the two men gauge the gravity of ALISON's statement.)*

ALEC. They look...they look kind of like a big city in the sky, don't they?

ALISON. Or a face moving behind a veil?

JERRY. Or a big bowl of soup.

ALISON. Jerry...

JERRY. Well they do! Kinda steaming on the top? When you're sitting at the table, waiting for Grace?

ALEC. Like a bath.

JERRY. Yeah, like when you're sitting in the bath, and the cool air is coming in the window...

ALEC. Did you ever used to suck on your washcloth?

JERRY *(a little uncomfortable)*. Sort of, I guess, I don't know...

ALISON. I did that too!

ALEC. Why was that so much fun?

ALISON. I don't know!

ALEC. Just thinking about it, I can feel the feel of that cloth in my mouth and the water, sucking it through the cloth like that. It felt so—

JERRY *(after a pause, an admission)*. Safe.

ALEC. Yeah! Safe. But why should that feel safe?

JERRY. Oral fixation of some sort, probably.

ALEC. I never thought of that.

ALISON. *I* used to lay the washcloth flat on the top of the water...and then watch it sink.

JERRY. Me too!

ALISON. No way!

ALEC. I did too!

ALISON. I thought that was just my thing.

JERRY. No, I did that all the time, darlin', I was like the pro.

ALEC. Well, maybe you were the *regional* pro, but I could get it to float for over a minute up here, so—

JERRY. What size washcloth are we talkin' about, though?

ALEC. Any size you want.

ALISON *(admonishment)*. You guys!

JERRY. I'm just saying...

ALEC. I would do that over and over again, that thing with the washcloth?...and my dad...

ALISON. My dad would be standing there shaving, I can see him...

JERRY. My dad'd be in the other room listening to the game.

ALEC *(like dropping a bomb)*. Well, *my* dad would sit there and play the accordion.

JERRY. No!

ALEC. Yes!

ALISON. In the bathroom?! Alec!

ALEC. He did! He played while I sat in the tub. It was his...I don't know what it was...it was...

JERRY. Weird!

ALEC. Yeah, it was weird.

ALISON. Was he good?

ALEC. He was OK. He doesn't play anymore. Not since my mom died.

JERRY. My mom's dead too.

ALEC. Sorry.

JERRY. It's OK, it's not your fault. *(Brief pause. They all take bites of their apples and think about death.)* I didn't mean what I said back there, darlin', about you—

ALISON. Yeah you did. *(After a beat.)* But that's OK.

ALEC. And I didn't—

ALISON. I know, Alec. I know. *(Brief pause. Exasperated:)* God.
JERRY. What?
ALISON. Nothing. *(Brief pause.)*
ALEC. You know what?
ALISON. What?
ALEC. This is gonna sound really stupid.
ALISON. Just say it.
ALEC. If President Kennedy—
JERRY. God rest his soul.
ALEC. God rest his soul. If President Kennedy came down right now in a spaceship? And we could go with him? *(Brief pause.)* I'd go.
JERRY. Me too.
ALISON. Me too. *(Brief pause.)*
JERRY. You're really gonna go back home, darlin'?
ALISON. Yeah, Jerry, and let's not talk about it, please?
ALEC. I could give you a ride to the train station. If you want.
ALISON. Uh...
JERRY. In the hearse?
ALEC. Yeah.
JERRY. Whoo.
ALISON. I don't know.
ALEC. With Jerry?
ALISON. That could be OK. *(To JERRY.)* Yeah? Jerry? You want to ride in a hearse?
JERRY. With you? I could do that, I guess.
ALEC. Good.
JERRY. By choice.
ALEC. Yeah.
JERRY. Good to do it once by choice.
ALEC. Yeah.

JERRY. No head.

ALEC. No head.

ALISON. Thanks, Alec. That'll be nice. We'll go to the station together. *(Pointing at the sky.)* Oh, did you see that?

JERRY. Yeah.

ALEC. Yeah.

ALISON. Wow. *(Brief pause.)* God, it looks so peaceful up there, doesn't it? It feels...it feels like we're standing at the edge of the universe, you know? Like this moment right here is a ledge. And we're looking out at the sea. The sea of everything that's just...about...to happen. *(Brief pause. ALISON takes a bite of apple.)* Listen, you guys, what if we all lived together?

JERRY. What do you mean?

ALISON. Nothing, I just mean—while I was packing I was thinking, what if we could all live together? On Alec's flower farm?

ALEC. All three of us?

ALISON. Yeah. *(To ALEC.)* That way, see, I wouldn't have to live at home, and you could be with me, and *(To JERRY.)* you could stay in the Coast Guard and visit whenever you wanted, and then when you got out of the service, you could come live with me and the baby and Alec and who knows?

JERRY. You and the baby and Alec.

ALISON. Yeah. And who knows?

JERRY. What do you mean, "who knows"?

ALISON. I just mean, wouldn't it be cool if it worked...if that could work? It was just an idea, I don't really mean anything by it, I'm going home. *(Long pause.)*

ALEC. And not marry either one of us, you mean?

ALISON. Right.

JERRY *(trying to understand)*. So—

ALEC. I couldn't live with you as a friend, though, I don't think, if that's what you're saying—

ALISON. It's not.

ALEC. Or even—

JERRY. It's not?

ALEC. —you know, as—

ALISON. Alec—

ALEC. I couldn't. I just couldn't. With him always coming around?

JERRY. Oh yeah, maybe you'd like it better if I just died!

ALISON. Jerry!

JERRY. All grey!

ALISON. Jerry!

JERRY. Well, that's what he's saying, isn't it?

ALEC. No, I'm saying she's in love with YOU! She just doesn't want to be alone! *(Brief pause.)*

ALISON. I know it's impossible, you guys. It was just an idea. Forget it. *(Long pause.)* What's in the box?

ALEC. Oh. My Audubon guidebooks.

ALISON. Oh, wow! From your mom!

ALEC. Yeah, I thought your baby might want them or something, to look at, you know...they're kind of interesting and I don't think I'll ever...you know...

ALISON. Can I see?

ALEC. Of course, they're yours. And Jerry's, I mean, sort of...whatever you want. They're yours. *(She takes the box and opens it, pulls out a guidebook.)*

ALISON. Wildflowers.

JERRY. You know, Alec, I've seen flowers in the South Pacific that'd make you wet your pants they're so pretty!

ALEC. I bet.

JERRY. You should never have been messing with that other stuff anyway, that's bad magic.

ALEC. Down at... *my* farm, there's this whole field of blue flag iris that just grew there wild out behind the barn. It's not much to look at now, but in the spring, boy, it's gonna be something.

JERRY. You really like flowers, don't you?

ALEC. You know... I do.

JERRY. Why?

ALEC. I don't know... maybe it's because... they do their thing, you know? They grow.

ALISON *(pointing in the book)*. Do they have these up here?

ALEC. Indian pipe? Yeah.

ALISON. It's kinda spooky-looking, isn't it?

JERRY. Looks kinda like a mushroom.

ALEC *(handing him a guidebook)*. Here's the mushroom book if you're interested.

JERRY. Thanks.

ALISON *(pulling another book from the box)*. Butterflies.

ALEC. Yeah. There's one in there. Look on page sixty.

JERRY. I had an uncle who died from eating a mushroom once. Amanita?

ALEC. That'd do it.

ALISON *(having found the page)*. Sara Orange Tip?

ALEC. Yeah. *(Tenderly.)* That's you.

ALISON. What's that supposed to mean?

ALEC. I don't know. To me that's always been you. *(Brief pause.)*

JERRY. I can see that.

ALEC. Don'tcha, kinda?

JERRY. Yeah.

ALEC *(suddenly)*. It's fine with me. *(Brief pause.)*

JERRY. Well, goddamn it, if it's fine with him, I guess it could be fine with me too.

ALISON. No, it can't ever work out, I know that, I just thought—

JERRY. No, it's good!

ALISON. It is?

ALEC. I like it.

ALISON *(surprised)*. We could fight all night the other way, I mean, but—

ALEC. Why?

ALISON. Exactly! I'm sure no one will think it can work. No one older anyway. But who cares what they think? They've screwed up everything anyway.

ALEC. Right.

JERRY. Right. *(Brief pause.)*

ALISON. So that's it?

ALEC. That's it.

JERRY. That's it.

ALISON. That's good.

(Lights out. Lights rise on a bright snowy morning in the orchard, a week later. ROSS and CINDY, in winter coats, are there.)

ROSS *(not grave—gossipy!)*. She's dead!

CINDY. Who's dead? *(Brief pause.)*

ROSS. May Whipstadt!

CINDY. No!

ROSS. Yes! And the sheriff's got Dwayne Lund in the lockup for suspicion of Mafia connections...and murder!

CINDY. He thinks Dwayne killed her?

ROSS. He doesn't know! He's scouring Dwayne's little apartment above the Sandwich Hut for evidence!

CINDY. Jesus, Mary and Joseph!

ROSS. I know it! But, Cindy, he's left her in the garage like he usually does. There's no way I'm gonna be able to get her up onto the table alone... I'm liable to break my hip again! I can't run this business without Alec, Cindy, what am I going to do?

CINDY. Ross—

ROSS. See, I should never have listened to you, Cindy, I should never have let Alec come out here! Four generations of Willoughby morticians—

CINDY. Ross, did it ever occur to you maybe it's time the Willoughbys got out of the funeral business?

ROSS. Oh, you sound just like my wife! Just like Ruth. She never wanted Alec to join me in the business either, and you know what? I bet this is all her revenge! Oh... I can't believe he's gone. And living with her! And him! And growing flowers! Jiminy Christmas, Cindy, I feel like I'm watching Rome burn!

CINDY. Ross, it's gonna be OK. Maybe... maybe you could move out here with me and Lindy and... who knows?

ROSS *(shocked)*. Cindy!

CINDY. I'm just teasing with you, Ross.

ROSS *(almost a little disappointed)*. Oh. *(After a beat.)* It's not as if my own life hasn't been plagued with doubts, you know. You don't think so probably, but it has.

CINDY. What kind of doubts?

ROSS. Oh, you know, the normal ones. About love and life and how you're supposed to behave considering everything's so beautiful...and there's so little time. *(Brief pause.)* Oh, by the way, I heard about your art gallery.

CINDY. What art gallery?

ROSS. Oh cripes! Maybe I'm ruining something?

CINDY. No, what is it, Ross? Just tell me. *(We hear a car pulling away, beeping its horn, and LINDY saying "Goodbye!" offstage.)*

ROSS. Well, it's—

CINDY. Just tell me!

ROSS. Nothing! It's just...I heard that Lindy bought Angry Dennis' old laundromat and you and Pam Schmit were gonna turn it into an art gallery. Maybe I'm mistaken.

CINDY. Who'd you hear that from?

ROSS. May Whipstadt. *(Sadder.)* Last time we talked.

(LINDY enters, holding an apple.)

LINDY. I just met...an astronaut! A real live astronaut! He doesn't know if he's gonna go to the moon or not yet, but he might, he really might! And I met him! And he's gonna give me money for my apples! Isn't that something? Damn, the air is nice today! Ross, I want to buy two caskets, *(To CINDY.)* and with the rest of the money, you know what, I figure we'll—what's the matter, Ross, why do you have that look on your face? Life's better than you think! *(Music rises. Lights fade.)*

END OF PLAY